the art of food

mushrooms

Conceived, written and designed by Sharon Plant and Ian E Wood
Published by Aspects Publishing, part of Aspects of Creativity
P.O.Box 65015, London N5 9BB

www.aspectsofcreativity.com
www.theartoffood.co.uk
For sales email sales@theartoffood.co.uk
For information email sharon@theartoffood.co.uk

the art of food

This book is accurate and true to the best of the abilities of the authors. The authors cannot accept responsibility for mistakes within it, or for the consequences thereof.

ISBN: 978-0-9568009-0-9

This is one of a series of books about the facts, fiction and fokelore of food. It is designed to give you delicious food for the table and delightful food for thought. With it you can create meals of interest and humour to feed the mind as well as the body.

Others in the series include the facts and folklore of offal, the wonder of colour in food, and the pleasures of chocolate.

This book gives you the facts, fiction and fokelore about...

mushrooms

contents

14 History
15 Collecting
19 Identification
23 Science
26 Music
27 Poisoning
28 Humour
29 Shrooms
30 Art
32 Facts
34 Quiz
38 Recipes
55 Thanks

history

The British fascination for all things fungal began in October 1868, when the Woolhope Naturalists' Field Club in Hereford held an event it called 'a foray amongst the funguses'. The event was a huge success, culminating in a banquet of mushrooms.

The enthusiasm for both the collecting and the cooking led to this becoming an annual gathering, attended by leading botanists, horticulturalists and geologists, each keen to sample and discover new varieties and tastes. The idea caught on elsewhere, particularly, for some reason, in Yorkshire!

By 1895 there were enough local enthusiasts to form a national society, the British Mycology Society. Every year since then, the society has organised fungal sorties in spring and autumn, and for a while they even held an annual truffle hunt.

This book acknowledges some of our leading mushroom specialists. After some high profile cases of poisoning, and with conservation authorities on guard against over-picking, it is time to stand up for mushrooming, says Peter Marren, author of *Mushrooms.*

There is a country code for collecting mushrooms that restricts us to picking 1.5kg of fungi, and many nature and heritage bodies ban collecting completely on their land. Some forests have introduced one-day licenses so that they can control both the quantity picked and the number of pickers.

The season's plenty varies, every third year or so is often good, but there is perhaps a fabulous harvest only once a decade. The weather plays a major role, and a fine balance of sun, rain and mildness is required to produce the bumper crop.

1.5kg and no more

collecting

brain food

Mushrooms are the fruit body of the plant, not the plant itself. The main organism, the mycelium, is a large underground network of fine threads that survives having its crop picked. Many scientists assert that mushrooms are the biggest things that have ever lived on the earth. In the Blue Mountains of eastern Oregon USA, a mycelium was found estimated to cover over 2,200 acres and be at least 2,400 years old. So, not fresh then.

Over the mushroom appetiser, you could dispute this. Some scientists say the largest organism is the Great Barrier Reef, while others believe it is the Pando Forest in Utah, a stand of genetically identical trees connected by a single root system.

in the wild

Mushrooms are in season pretty much all year round but certain varieties come into their own at particular times.

January	chestnut mushrooms
April / May	morels, St George's mushroom
June	St George's mushroom
July	chanterelles, summer truffles, chicken of the woods
August	ceps (aka porcini), chanterelles, field mushrooms, horse mushrooms, oyster mushrooms (pleurottes), parasols, puffballs, giant shaggy ink caps, summer truffles, chicken of the woods
September	ceps, chanterelles, field, horse, oyster, parasols, puffballs, giant shaggy ink caps, summer truffles
October	chestnuts, chanterelles, hedgehog fungus, horse, oyster, parasols, puffballs, giant shaggy ink caps, summer truffles, wood blewits
November	chestnuts, hedgehog fungus, horse, oyster, wood blewits
December	chestnut mushrooms

a sense of smell

As with all food, smell is significant, and sometimes vital. The importance of not tasting the mushrooms you find cannot be stressed enough, unless you really know your mushrooms, or you are foraging with an expert, and even experts taste only a tiny bit and then spit. However, another means of identification and gratification is available; our sense of smell.

Fungi are said to have a wider range of aroma than flowers, including the smell of curry, radish, marzipan, aniseed, swimming pools and freshly dug potatoes. And experts say, it does what it says on the packet: if it smells of ink, it will taste of ink, although we'd like to meet the man who checked this out.

There are also hot-tasting varieties, said to be much favoured by the Finns but less popular in Britain where we enjoy somewhat milder concoctions.

brain food

Must reads: *Mushrooms* by Roger Philips; *Mushrooms: River Cottage Handbook* by John Wright; *Mushrooms* by Peter Marren; and *Complete Mushroom Book: The Quiet Hunt* by Antonio Carluccio

identification

There are some very good identification books but if you go out mushrooming bear in mind that for every edible species there is as likely to be an inedible look alike. The excellent Blusher is easily mistaken for the sinister Panther Cap, so if in doubt, avoid.

When identifying mushrooms please note that the difference between a toadstool and a mushroom is none.

1. Toadstools and mushrooms are the same and no scientific distinction exists between them
2. You cannot define either by shape, colour or appearance since there is no standard differentiation between them
3. Toadstools and mushrooms are not defined by their level of toxicity: anything classed as either may be nontoxic, mildly toxic, hallucinogenic or extremely poisonous

brain food

The Oak Milkcap was rarely eaten because it was said to smell of bedbugs. Mushroom enthusiast John Wright said it smelt even more of carrots, and a new edible mushroom was born.

brain food

Folklore – if it peels, it's okay; if a squirrel has eaten it, you can too. But folks beware; the fearsome Death Cap is often well nibbled.

common uk edibles

chestnut

shiitake

oyster

flat

button

please try this at home

We sat the family round the table and conducted a tasting of raw and cooked common edibles and asked for silence because one taster said 'the noise is interfering with my taste buds'. We asked the kids to taste different mushrooms and write down what they thought, so in silence we discovered...

Button mushrooms: were described as tasting like 'a nut that I've never tasted before', while another taster said, 'I'm tasting KitKat!' He has a sweet tooth.

Portobello mushrooms: were admired for their texture: 'the inside is corky, nice'. Another taster said she was getting an exciting mix of earth, air and soil.

Chestnut mushrooms: one taster said, 'I'm getting vanilla, with the underside of logs', another thought they were 'marmitey'. A third felt they were calm, subtle and elegant.

Shiitake mushrooms: one taster told us 'they're chewy, a bit like tough jelly, octopus without the fish', while another said she could taste 'vegetables, mainly spinach'.

Oyster mushrooms: one of our tasters got 'a hint of a newly emulsioned room'. But, another described them as 'delicate and feminine', and yet another said they were fragranced, 'coming from a world of their own'. And finally, 'I can taste flowers, hedgerows and mulch'.

Black summer truffles: 'taste of earth!'.

mar-mitey

octo-pus with-out the fish

classification

When classifying mushrooms we look for a series of comparable elements. These include: size, shape, texture, colour, flesh, stipe ring, taste, smell, gills, habitat, chemicals and spores.

The cap shape might be flattened, bell-shaped or conical, or another shape all together, and its texture might be cracking, shaggy, smooth or wrinkled, again, amongst other things. How the gills are attached and the arrangement of the gills also helps identification. The stipe shape might be tapering, rooting or club shaped and it might be shaggy, smooth or scaly. There is no end to the possibilities and variations, and as a result, no end to the mistakes that you can make.

However, the main groups have been classified as: boletes, milkcaps, parasols, amanita, waxcaps, honey fungus, knights, cavaliers, funnels, toughshanks, parachutes, blewits, bonnets, shields, rustgills, tufts, scalycaps, mushrooms (interestingly), inkcaps, oysters, corals, puffballs, saddles, morels and cups... amongst others. Simple.

gill fungi

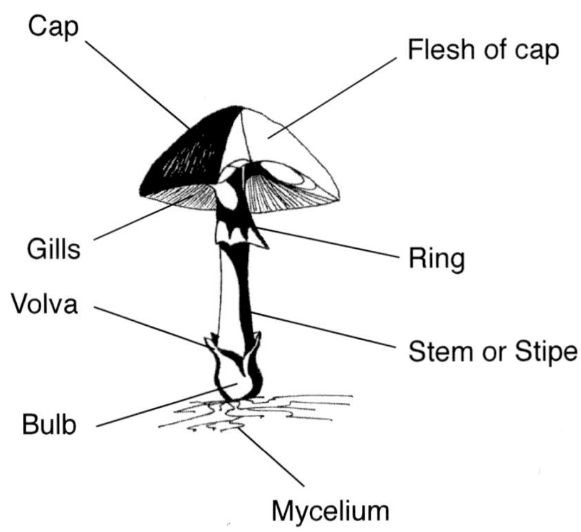

pore fungi

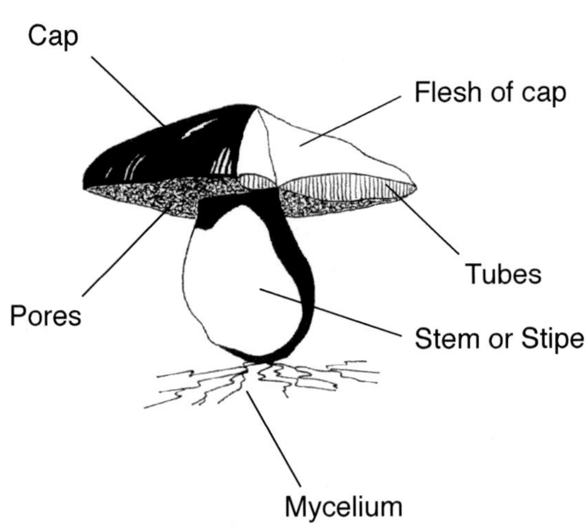

fungi save the world

Paul Stamets, a scientist working in Washington State, is a leading mycologist and has come up with six ways in which mushrooms might save the world. The focus of his research is the mycelium, the one-cell thick network that forms the vast structure underground.

1. Cleaning polluted water: oyster mushroom mycelium is grown in wood chips inside a sack, which is placed in the path of polluted water. The upstream side of the sack soaks up the pollution providing a 100:1 reduction in bacteria

2. Solving insect infestations: insects pick up the mycelium on leaves and other foodstuffs, carry it to the nest, and the nest becomes infected and destroyed

3. Fuel: he can make ethanol out of mycelium

4. Grow your own forest: this comes in a ready impregnated box, just add soil and plants sprout

5. Defense: mycelium breaks down nerve gas components. VX is one of the world's deadliest chemical weapons. In a Department of Defense test, rare mushroom strains ate nerve gas molecules leaving the neurotoxins safe for the environment and for humans

6. Medicine: working with others he has successfully shown how mycelium can treat bacterial infections such as tuberculosis and smallpox

Go to www.TED.com and find out more.

music

Imagine your kids, X-Factor hopefuls, in a garage where, instead of developing their music skills, they wile away the hours trying to find the name for the band that will grant them access to stardom, riches and girls. They will decide that this name has to be different, anarchic, and slightly metaphysical, and above all it will be an idea that no one has had before. They decide they will call it 'mushroom' or a derivative thereof.

Sadly, there are over sixty published bands with mushroom in their name, so the number that have used the name and failed must be many hundreds more.

Some of the least imaginative include; Mushroom, Mushrooms, Mushroomers and Magick Mushroom Band. Better marks might be given to; Mushroom Pillow, In the Summer of the Mushroom Honey, The Mixtape Philosophies of Mushroom Black and our favourite; Mushroom's Patience. For album titles the list is as long, but considerably less imaginative.

some mushroom bands
are quite unsavoury

poisoning

Before the glamour of CSI, before medicine became a little more scientific than leeches, when someone inexplicably popped their clogs, especially someone famous, those around would whisper, 'mushroom poisoning'. As a result lots of famous people might have died, deliberately or accidently, from mushroom poisoning. Or they might not. Some such persons deemed to have suffered this fate include:

1. Buddha (Siddhartha Gautama)
2. Pope Clement VII
3. Holy Roman Emperor Charles VI
4. Tsarina Natalia Naryshkina, five years Tsarina of all Russia, mother of Peter the Great and a seriously ugly lady
5. Johann Schobert, harpsichordist and composer of hundreds of pieces for the... harpsichord
6. Alexander the Great, uniter of empires, conqueror of nations and slaughterer of millions
7. Both Emperor Claudius and his son Britannicus were poisoned; the throne being 'inherited' by Nero, the son of Claudius' doctor. Looks like a bit of a fiddle
8. Daniel Gabriel Fahrenheit; died of a mushroon induced fever. Ironic
9. Wolfgang Amadeus Mozart
10. Napoleon Bonaparte; though it could also have been the poisonous hair cream, the poisonous wallpaper or the poisonous arsenic later found in his hair
11. Robin Hood; how is it that there can be speculation about the death of a fictional character?
12. US President Zachary Taylor, but subsequent exhumation put the cause more probably as excess cherries and iced milk
13. More definitively, Horse Whisperer author Nicolas Evans, made the news again when he had mushroom poisoning. He survived and is considering writing a book about his experience called the 'Hoarse Whisperer.'

Daniel Gabriel Fahrenheit died of fever

humour

There is the one we all know that ends with, "... because he was a fungi (fun guy)!" Please don't tell that to anyone over five years old. There is the one that ends with, "... because there wasn't mushroom (much room)." The limit on that one is four years.

Seventy percent of mushroom jokes are a weak attempt to reframe these two weak plays on words. There is room for the invention of more, but not if you are sober or have refined guests, unless you can invent a play of words on volva, ring, cap, stalk that your guests will find hilarious. You could invite some ten year olds for a late supper.

The final 30% of jokes are based on:

"A woman announces to her friend that she is getting married for the fourth time.
"How wonderful! But I hope you don't mind me asking what happened to your first husband?"
"He ate poisonous mushrooms and died."
"Oh, how tragic! What about your second husband?"
"He ate poisonous mushrooms too and died."
"Oh, how terrible! I'm almost afraid to ask about your third husband."
"He died of a broken neck."
"A broken neck?"
"He wouldn't eat the mushrooms."

shrooms

'Magic mushrooms' or 'shrooms', the name derived from the eater's inability to form a coherent sentence, produce a variety of psychedelic effects. This is not to be confused with psychedelia, which relates to a well-known TV chef.

Magic mushrooms contain psilocin, also known as 4-hydroxyl-dimeth-yltryptamine, a name worth dropping into conversation if you feel confident. Over 200 species of mushroom contain psilocin and there is more in the caps than the stems. It is absorbed through the lining of the mouth and stomach and has some highly variable effects.

If you need to feel that what you see has profound meaning, if you are not happy with the usual colours and need some new ones, if you want to feel euphoria and want to take a risk, magic mushrooms are the way forward. But their effects are, as stated, highly variable, so you should also have a liking for uncontrolled twitching, a run away heart rate, deep, profound and extreme despair and hallucinations with your eyes closed and open. On the good side, there are reports of mystical or spiritual experiences. But before you seek God though mycological means, please note that in controlled experiments, over a third of users suffer extreme fear (dysphoria), and long-term effects can include violence, aggression, homicidal and suicidal attempts, prolonged schizophrenia-like psychosis and convulsions. Normal mushrooms are nice, stick with them, and they are legal.

In 2005 the law on magic mushrooms changed: mushrooms containing psilocin were cited under the Misuse of Drugs Act and are now class A drugs. Ten percent of convicted mushroom users end up doing porridge.

**'shrooms' are a Class A drug and 10%
of convicted users end up doing porridge**

STILL LIFE WITH A MONKEY — Jan Davidsz de Heen

STILL LIFE WITH MUSHROOMS AND BUTTERFLIES
Otto Marseus van Schrieck

MUSHROON HUNTING — Ivan Inaovich Shishkin

L'HOMME POTAGER
Guiseppe Arcimboldo

MUSHROOM AND ROWAN
Aleksandra Saikina

DRIED MUSHROOM TRIO
Faith Te

L'HOMME POTAGER
Guiseppe Arcimboldo

Mushrooms Biddy Hodon

mush
room
show
room

L'AUTOMNE
Guiseppe Arcimboldo

L'ETE *Guiseppe Arcimboldo*

A BASKET OF WILD MUSHROOMS
AND BLACKBERRIES *Jabez Bligh*

MUSHROOM PIKER *Kendall Kessler*

did you know?

Mushrooms have relatives, some of them undesirable and embarrassing: yeast, mildew and Athletes' Foot for example. Mushrooms are not plants: like animals and bacteria they have a taxonomic category all to themselves. They do not need light and they do not photosynthesise, they eat stuff. In the case of Athletes' Foot, they eat the Keratin in the skin between our toes, that is the same Keratin that beauty brands put in shampoo and skin care products. Mushrooms are the ultimate scavengers; they can eat oil, waste, sulphur and biological weapons, and so on down a very long menu.

About a billion years ago when the first unicellular life split into two evolutionary branches, one became plants and the other then split into mushrooms and, after quite a long time, animals and ultimately us. Mushrooms are therefore, in evolutionary terms, closer to animals than plants. Athletes' Foot, is therefore a cousin of cannibalism.

Two hundred and fifty million years ago, marking the boundary between the Permian and the Triassic geological periods, there was the 'mother of all mass extinctions,' also know as the 'Great Dying', in which between 50% and 95% of species, depending upon where they lived, were wiped out. The cause of this ultimate wipe out may have been the impact of a meteor, volcanic activity or an imbalance in the gases in the atmosphere, but as a result, for tens of millions of years, fungi were Earth's dominant life-form.

The structure of fungi, the stuff that holds them together and gives them the texture in the mouth, is Chitin (pronounced Kite-In). Because of their evolutionary past, this is the same substance that forms the structures of insects and crustaceans, for example, exoskeletons of beetles and beaks of squid. Chitin is a relative of Keratin that performs the same structural function in reptiles, amphibians and mammals: fur, talons, claws, fingernails and hair.

brain food

Hairdressing and pedicures are a form of Keratin maintenance and were it not for a few evolutionary divergences, eating mushrooms would be akin to chewing your nails, but don't let that stop you enjoying them.

People who collect mushrooms for consumption are known as mycophagists, and the act of collecting them for consumption is known as mushroom hunting, or simply mushrooming.

China is the world's largest edible mushroom producer. The country produces about half of all cultivated mushrooms, and around 2.7kgs (6lb) of mushrooms is consumed per year by over a billion people. Edible mushrooms are used extensively in Chinese, Korean, European and Japanese cuisines.

Many species are high in dietary fibre, protein and vitamins such as thiamine, riboflavin, niacin, biotin, and ascorbic acid. Though not normally a significant source of vitamin D, some mushrooms can become significant sources after exposure to ultraviolet light, which also darkens their skin. Mushrooms are also a source of minerals, including selenium, potassium and phosphorus.

Most mushrooms sold in supermarkets have been commercially grown on mushroom farms. The most popular of these, Agaricus Bisporus, is generally considered safe for most people to eat because it is grown in controlled, sterilised environments, though some people do not tolerate it well. Several varieties of Agaricus Bisporus are grown commercially, including whites, crimini and portobello. Other cultivated species now available at many grocers include shiitake, maitake or hen-of-the-woods, oyster and enoki.

brain food

Before offering your guests your favourite mushroom dish, read John Lanchester's Debt to Pleasure, a superb romp through misadventure and madness of the culinary persuasion.

quiz

1. Which civilisation claimed the mushroom was the plant of immortality?
2. It is said that the addition of mushrooms adds an umami lift to food. What is umami?
3. What is the common name for Amanita Phalloides, responsible for 90% of deaths caused by fungus poisoning world-wide?
4. What is the common name for mushrooms that smell of rotting meat, attracting flies that disperse their spores?
5. How much cholesterol does a mushroom have?
6. Name any minerals and vitamins found in mushrooms.
7. Name four ways of preserving mushrooms.
8. What are the three main controlled elements of a mushroom 'farm'?
9. What are magic mushrooms?
10. Which fungi is used to start fires?

1. The Egyptian

2. Umami is the fifth taste sensation (after sweet, sour, bitter and salty) discovered in Japan in 1906 at Tokyo University

3. The Death Cap

4. Stinkhorns

5. None

6. Selenium, potassium, copper, iron, niacin, B-complex vitamins (riboflavin, niacin, pantothenic acid). One portobello mushroom generally has more potassium than a banana.

7. Drying, canning, pickling, freezing

8. Airflow, temperature and light are constantly monitored in mushroom growing buildings

9. There are around 12 different varieties of magic mushroom growing throughout the UK that have a powerful hallucinogenic effect similar to LSD. The main type is called Liberty Cap Psilocybe. The other more potent variety is the Amanita Muscaria

10. The tinder fungi

yin and yang soup

mushroom soup

50g butter
1 medium onion (finely diced)
250g chestnut mushrooms (washed and sliced)
4 tbsp flour
425ml chicken stock
150ml milk
1 tbsp chopped parsley
50ml cream
Salt and pepper

1. Melt butter and fry onion until soft, not brown
2. Add mushrooms, flour, fry for 5 minutes
3. Remove from heat, slowly add stock, stirring continuously
4. Return to heat, bring to boil, stirring until it thickens
5. Stir in the milk and the parsley
6. Puree in blender until smooth, soup can be refrigerated for 24 hours
7. Return to pan, reheat, season to taste
8. Just before plating up, remove from heat, stir in cream

plating up

Warm 4 soup bowls
Put soups into separate jugs
Simultaneously pour both soups slowly from opposite sides of each bowl
Garnish watercress half with a watercress leaf
Garnish mushroom half with parsley
Serve immediately

watercress soup

6 bunches watercress (trim base from stalks, chop roughly)
1 large potato (peeled, finely chopped)
3 tsp olive oil
1 litre boiling water
1.5 tsp sea salt
100ml cream
Freshly ground pepper

1. Heat oil to sizzling, add cress and potato, stirring rapidly
2. Stir for ½ minute until cress is just wilting
3. Pour in boiling water, season to taste
4. Reduce to simmer, cook until potato is soft and almost melted into soup (about 15mins)
5. Puree until smooth
6. Cool and chill quickly to retain colour
7. When ready to use, put in pan, bring to boil whisking steadily
8. Check seasoning

button mushroon sauce

serves 4 to 6

80g button mushrooms (sliced)
1 tbsp butter
125ml chicken stock
250ml double cream
Salt and pepper

1. Sweat the mushrooms in the butter for 3 minutes
2. Add the stock and reduce by half
3. Add the cream and reduce by a third
4. Season with salt and pepper
5. Puree to satin smooth
6. Reheat and serve

portobello mushroon pie

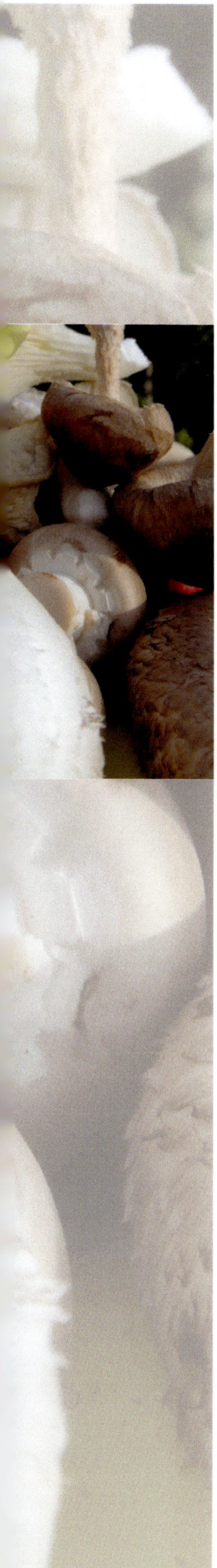

serves 4 to 6

175g packet rough puff pastry
25g butter
2 medium onions (finely chopped)
2 or 3 large Portobello mushrooms (peeled and thickly sliced)
1 tbsp butter (melted)
1 tsp salt
0.25 tsp black pepper
150ml double cream
0.25 tsp cayenne pepper
1.5 tsp dried oregano
1 oz pinenuts
3 oz pancetta
4 hard-boiled eggs (sliced)
A little milk

1. Preheat oven to 200^{0}C
2. In large frying pan melt butter, when foam subsides add onions, cook until translucent, transfer to pie dish
3. Add pancetta and fry gently (3 mins)
4. Arrange mushrooms and pancetta on top of onions, coat with melted butter
5. Sprinkle on the pinenuts
6. Season with $^1/_2$ tsp salt and half the pepper
7. Pour cream on top, sprinkle with remaining salt and pepper, cayenne and oregano
8. Top with slices of hard-boiled egg
9. On a floured surface, roll out dough to 2.5cms larger than pie dish
10. Trim edges, roll again and cut a narrow strip, dampen pie dish rim, press dough strip on top, lightly moisten strip
11. Lift dough lid onto the dish, trim and crimp edges to seal
12. Cut a large cross in the centre, brush top with milk
13. Bake for 30mins or until pastry is golden

Notes:
Mushrooms release juices during cooking so there is no need to add extra liquid. Mushrooms also shrink, so pile them high. For later use, the pie will stand a gentle reheat in the microwave without going too floppy.

stuffed field mushrooms

serves 4

The field mushroom, Agaricus Campestris, is the most commonly eaten wild mushroom in Britain. Its species name Campestris is derived from the Latin word campus, which means field, and it is seen most commonly in meadows grazed by horses, cattle or sheep. It can be found worldwide and appears in grassy areas after rain from late summer through autumn. It is fast maturing and has a short shelf-life.

8 field mushrooms
2 tbsp olive oil, plus extra for greasing
4 shallots (finely chopped)
120g pinenuts (toasted)
4 tbsp basil (torn)
4 tbsp parsley (finely chopped)
Salt and freshly ground black pepper
175g goat's cheese
8 slices Pancetta

1. Preheat the oven to 190°C
2. Place the mushrooms on oiled baking tray
3. Heat olive oil in a large frying pan and fry the shallots over a medium heat for 2–3 minutes, or until softened, stirring frequently
4. Add pinenuts, basil, parsley, and season to taste
5. Spoon mixture into the mushrooms, top with a slice of goat's cheese
6. Wrap a slice of pancetta around each mushroom, tucking ends underneath
7. Bake for 15–20 minutes, or until the mushrooms are tender and the pancetta is crisp
8. Serve immediately

portobello mushroom risotto

serves 4

1 onion (chopped)
1 leek (thinly sliced)
225g portobello mushrooms (thinly sliced)
75g back bacon (optional but nice)
1 lemon, juice and rind (peel off rind in a large swirl)
60ml white wine
350g long grain rice
1 tbsp olive oil
1 litre chicken stock
125g hard cheese (grated)
Salt and pepper

1. Boil the chicken stock in a large saucepan and turn down to simmer
2. Heat oil in a large heavy based saucepan, add onion, bacon, leek and 2 tbsps water
3. Cook for 2-3mins or until the mixture begins to soften
4. Stir in rice, season
5. Add wine, lemon rind, 2 tbsps lemon juice and two tbsps stock
6. Cook gently, stirring occasionally, until the wine and stock is absorbed
7. Add mushrooms and gradually add simmering liquid, a spoonful at a time
8. Let mixture absorb the stock before adding next spoonful
9. Keep stirring and adding stock
10. When most of the stock has been added and the rice is creamy, add cheese and stir until the cheese begins to melt
11. Remove the lemon rind and season to taste
12. Serve with salad or rocket leaves and a drizzle of olive oil

flat mushroom lasagne

serves 4

2 garlic cloves (crushed)
3 oz butter
4 large flat mushrooms (quartered)
1 large squash, thinly sliced (pumpkin or butternut are alternatives; adjust the amount accordingly
300g red peppers (pips removed, sliced)
3 tbsp tomato paste
1 tsp oregano
Salt and pepper
10 oz cheddar cheese
4 large tomatoes (chopped)
1 tsp paprika
6 lasagne sheets
2 onions
Cream

1. Pre-heat oven to 190°C
2. Soften onions and vegetables in olive oil for 15 mins on high heat, stirring continuously
3. Add tomatoes, paprika, oregano, garlic, tomato paste and bring to boil. Season.
4. Place alternate layers of vegetables drizzled with cream and pasta sheets in oven proof dish, finishing with a layer of vegetables
5. Top with cheese
6. Bake for 30mins, or until golden brown

field mushroom and potato dauphinoise

serves 4

4 large field mushrooms (sliced)
Butter
1kg floury potatoes (peeled and thinly sliced)
150ml milk
300ml double cream
Half a garlic clove (crushed)
Salt and pepper
Buttered baking dish

1. Heat oven to 180°C
2. Cook mushrooms in butter until softened
3. Heat milk and double cream with garlic
4. Add potato slices, season, simmer for 5mins
5. Allow to cool, layer potatoes and mushrooms in dish
6. Pour liquid over dish, bake for 1.5 hours until golden
7. Leave for 15mins before serving

pork loin steak with chanterelles and sweetbread custard

serves 4

The North West of Britain has a reputation for basic foods such as fish and chips, tripe and black pudding, but this recipe, from a Windermere cook, shows an alternative offering. With such local wonders as flitter picnics (limpets), tiny queenies (sweet scallops), skate nobs and sly cakes, this reputation is clearly ill-founded.

custard

1 med onion (finely chopped)
1 tbsp oil
30g butter
175g sweetbreads (blanched, cleaned, cut into 1cm cubes)
1 egg
2 egg yolks
300ml double cream

Cook the custard first

1. Cook the onion gently in the oil and butter until soft (do not colour onion)
2. Add sweetbreads heating them through
3. Divide between 4 well-buttered dariole moulds
4. Beat eggs, egg yolks and 2/3 of the cream together, season
5. Pour over sweetbreads to fill the moulds, cover
6. Stand in a bain marie and poach at 180°C until set, (25 mins)

pork

4 pork loin steaks
3 tbsp oil
90g butter
125g chanterelles (rinsed and diced)
Sprig of fresh thyme (discard stalk)
4 tbsp Madeira
4 tbsp dry white wine
Salt & pepper

Cook chanterelles and pork

1. Fry the pork steaks in oil and $\frac{1}{2}$ of the butter on both sides
2. When brown outside but pink inside, remove, cover. Keep warm
3. Add chanterelles and thyme leaves to pan. Saute fast until cooked
4. Pour in Madeira and flame
5. Add wine and reduce a little
6. Cut remaining butter into small pieces and add; swirl around pan, remove before sauce oils
7. Serve the pork surrounded by the chanterelles
8. Turn out custards, top each with teaspoon of cream

white cup mushroom puffs

serves 4

12 white cup mushrooms
250g frozen puff pastry sheets (defrosted)
15g butter
½ tsp marjoram
Freshly ground black pepper
1 egg (lightly beaten)

1. Unroll the pastry sheets
2. Using a 7.5 cm fluted round cutter, cut out 24 pastry rounds
3. Place one mushroom, stalk side up, on each of 12 pastry circles
4. Put a small knob of butter, a pinch of marjoram and a sprinkling of pepper on each mushroom.
5. Brush the edges of each mushroom-topped pastry circle with beaten egg
6. Place a second circle of pastry on top
7. Bring together the pastry edges, pressing well to seal. Flute the edges.
8. Dampen 2 baking sheets and transfer the puffs to them. Cover the puffs with clingfilm and refrigerate for 15mins
9. Heat oven to 220°C
10. Brush tops with the remaining beaten egg
11. Bake for 10-15mins until well-risen and golden brown
12. Serve immediately with dressed salad

field mushroom and feta quesadilla

serves 4

They trail in from school, tired and scrappy, each trying to describe to you the worst element of their day and all talking at once. Your best diversion is the smell of this mushroom and feta quesadilla, during the eating of which you will have time to ask if any good things happened during the day.

6 field mushrooms (sliced)
200g feta cheese (crumbled)
Half a red onion (thinly sliced)
Coriander (chopped)
6 flour tortilla
Butter

1. Soften onions in butter
2. Add mushrooms until softened, remove from heat
3. Mix cheese with mushrooms and onions and put aside
4. Put first tortilla in non-stick frying pan
5. Top with a couple of spoonfuls of the mushroom mix, put a second tortilla on top
6. Press down until cheese melts and sticks tortillas together and the bottom is golden
7. Flip over and brown other side
8. Repeat with other tortillas until mixture used up
9. Cut into wedges and serve

cooking with puffballs

Some people refer to puffballs as breakfast mushrooms because they go so nicely with eggs, but they can also be served as a thick mushroom steak that develops a lovely, golden colour when browned in butter.

Puffballs range in size from a marble to a medicine ball; their surfaces can be smooth, covered with small or round warts, or ornamented with spikes. They are usually white and round and attached to the ground with little or no apparent stem.

Assuming you have obtained reliable puffballs, you should still consider these points before eating: when cut, the puffball must be all white inside, any shade of yellow or purple makes them upsetting or inedible, and they must have a uniform internal consistency. Before cooking, clean, dry and peel off the outer layer.

1. Dip 1cm thick slices of puffball in a batter of egg and milk
2. Cover with fresh bread crumbs seasoned with salt and pepper
3. Saute in butter
4. Serve with a tangy sauce

If you have identified a particularly large puffball you can

1. Slice it thinly
2. Pan-sear it in butter
3. Roll it around crab meat, tuna, or other fillings of your choice
4. Hold in place with a toothpick
5. Bake for dinner party nibbles

shiitake, beef and red wine stew

The shiitake mushroom is perhaps the best known of the Japanese mushrooms and has a relatively strong flavour. It has a flattish cap with edges that curl under; the woody stem is a bit chewy and should be discarded. You can buy them fresh or dried, and if you like mushrooms with a kick, purchase the dried version, which must be rehydrated before cooking and again, the hard stem discarded after soaking. This dish is beautiful served on buttery, creamed, potato mash, garnished with flat leaf parsley.

serves 4 to 6

60ml vegetable oil
3 leeks (cut into 4cm lengths)
300g fresh shiitake mushrooms (stems off, cut in half if large)
1 large onion (chopped)
1 large carrot (peeled and chopped)
4 rashers streaky bacon (chopped)
2 tbsp plain flour
1 tsp ground pepper
Pinch sea salt
1kg stewing beef (cut into large cubes)
3 garlic cloves (crushed)
375ml red wine
375ml sake (or double red wine portion if you prefer)

1. Cook leeks until golden in 1tbs of vegetable oil, remove from pan
2. Add shiitake, cook for few minutes until slightly browned, set aside in leeks
3. Add onion, carrot and bacon to pan and cook for 10 mins
4. Toss the beef in the flour, salt and pepper
5. Add a little more oil to the pan and brown the beef in batches, set aside
6. Add garlic to pan, stir, add wine and sake, stir
7. Return beef to pan with bacon, onions and carrots, add 250ml water
8. Bring to the boil, reduce heat to low, cover, simmer for 1.5 hours
9. Add leeks and shiitake, cook uncovered for 30mins
10. Beef should be very tender and sauce thick